Mini Knitted Safari

Dedication

This book is dedicated to my mother.

Mini Knitted Safari

Sachiyo Ishii

Search Press

First published in Great Britain 2014

Search Press Limited
Wellwood, North Farm Road,
Tunbridge Wells, Kent TN2 3DR

Text copyright © Sashiyo Ishii, 2014

Photographs by Paul Bricknell at Search Press Studios

Photographs and design copyright © Search Press Ltd 2014

ISBN 978 1 84448 991 6

Suppliers
If you have difficulty in obtaining any of the materials and equipment mentioned in this book, then please visit the Search Press website for details of suppliers:
www.searchpress.com

You are invited to view the author's work at:
etsy.com/shop/sachiyoishii
visit her website at: knitsbysachi.com
visit her blog at: knitsbysachi.wordpress.com
search for KnitsbySachi on www.ravelry.com
or search for Knits by Sachi on Facebook

Printed in China

Acknowledgements

I would like to thank everyone in the Search Press team, especially Roz Dace and Sophie Kersey, for helping to bring my animals to life. Without you, this would not have been possible. Thanks also to Jacky Edwards for her expert pattern checking.

Contents

Elephant

Brown Bear

Polar Bear

Hippopotamus

Rhinoceros

Buffalo

Lion

Tiger

Tapir

Zebra

Impala

Gazelle

Giraffe

Monkey

Gorilla

Kangaroo

Koala

Panda

Meerkats

Penguin

Pelican

Toucan

Parrot

Vulture

Crocodile

Snake

Giant Turtle

Introduction

When I show my work to my friends, they all say I must have great patience. The truth is – I don't! That is why I create toys.

I took up knitting well into my thirties, after my second son was born. Never having held a knitting needle before, I started with baby knits of course, but I soon discovered that even to knit baby garments, you need to invest a lot of time and materials. This has its rewards, but I must admit I found knitting many stitches, row after row, rather boring. My first sweater was a disappointment. The stitches were very uneven and it had sleeves of different lengths. I didn't go to the trouble of making a gauge (or tension) sample, so it didn't even fit my son. This might be a classic case of a beginner being over-ambitious and failing to enjoy the craft itself, and this may sound familiar to some of you.

I still don't like making gauge samples, or working on the same project for days. Creating small toys gives me sense of accomplishment more quickly, but at the same time I can work towards a larger project, which is a collection of those creations, like this mini safari. I can have a short-term goal and a long-term goal.

There is something for everyone in this book. If you are new to knitting, start with the patchwork safari mat. You will be able to practise basic knitting and sewing skills. Then you can go on to the twenty-seven animal patterns. They are surprisingly simple, knitted flat and sewn together at the end. You do not need circular needles. Most share the same basic pattern, starting from the hind legs and finishing at the tip of the nose. Apart from a few exceptions, the limbs are knitted as you knit the body so that there is no need to knit each leg, head or arm and attach them at the end. Follow the basic step by step once, and the rest will come easily. Each animal requires very little yarn; around 10g (1/3oz). There is no need for glue, tape or pipe cleaners. It doesn't take too long to make one animal, and you don't have to worry about the gauge or size of the finished items too much. There are no rules, and so no mistakes. You might find the work a little fiddly and difficult at the beginning, but don't worry. You will improve your skills as you practise, and any work you produce will have a unique character anyway.

I have included some techniques and tips I use as a doll maker. If you are already an accomplished knitter but new to toy making, they might give you another dimension. You can make and collect your animals a few at a time, rather than all in one go, or just make your favourites. If you are more ambitious, make two of each animal to create a Noah's Ark scene. The mini safari can be a group project, too, for fundraising for example.

Crafts like knitting give you the chance to withdraw from your busy everyday life and be at peace with yourself. This can help you through difficult times. I hope you will enjoy this book as much as I have enjoyed creating it.

Happy knitting!

Materials and tools

Yarn

All the animals are knitted in double knitting, or DK, (8-ply) yarn. Make good use of your yarn stash if you have some already. You don't need a lot to create each animal; the average is 10g (1/3oz). Even the largest, which is the elephant, requires only 15g (1/2oz) of yarn.

I have used 100% wool throughout the projects with a very few exceptions. I find some synthetic yarns are bulky and difficult to knit with small needles, and quite often the results are disappointing. I love the feel of wool and the colour and tones it can create. If you are making animals as toys for children, you might wish to choose the most natural materials available. However, if you are allergic to natural sheep's wool, then choose cotton or synthetic yarns.

Embroidery or tapestry yarns are very helpful if you want small quantities of many different colours. Tapestry yarn is fairly tightly plied; it gives a clean, finished look, and it is 100% wool.

Use finer 2- or 3-ply embroidery yarn for manes and tails, or if you do not have these, you can take a couple of strands from DK yarn.

Stuffing

The animals are stuffed with uncarded washed wool fleece with fairly short fibres. This is ideal for stuffing small toys. It has plenty of bounce, fills the shapes and reaches into the tips of small parts. Some of these wools are naturally brown and very good for filling dark animals. Fill the animals a little at a time and tease the stuffing into place.

If you cannot get wool fleece, cotton wool is another good choice. Use it in the same way.

Polyester toy stuffing can be used too, but this can make it more difficult to fill small parts. For this reason, you could use cotton wool to fill in the tips of body parts, and use polyester toy filling to fill larger parts.

Quick guide to washing raw fleece

If you are lucky enough to lay your hands on raw fleece, you can use it for stuffing. It doesn't have to be the top quality. Short hair fleece which isn't suitable for spinning is best, as it has more bounce. However, untreated fleece is very oily and dirty. Here is a quick guide to how to wash it.

• Take a handful of fleece, an amount that will wash comfortably in a bucket.

• Brush off any plant debris.

• Wash the fleece with tepid warm water a few times.

• Soak it in warm water for a short while with a squirt of washing up liquid or cheap shampoo.

• Rinse with tepid water until the water runs clear.

• Put it in a laundry net and spin in your washing machine.

• Spread it out to dry.

• Fluff it out to get rid of any lumps and use it to fill your animals.

Needles

Double-pointed needles, size 2.75mm (UK 12/US 2) These are the basic needles that I used to create the animals. The knitted body of the animals needs to be tight so that the stuffing will not be visible. You may find it difficult to knit with the DK yarn on such fine needles, especially if you are new to toy making. If so, experiment with slightly larger needles. Also, if you are using synthetic yarn, which tends to be a little bulkier than wool, you might want to increase the needle size. The tension does not need to be defined for this project. You can be quite relaxed about the size. However, when you are making a set of animals as for this safari park scene, it is a good idea to use same size needles throughout, to keep the proportions right.

Crochet hook, size 3.25mm (UK 10/US D) or similar This is used for picking up stitches and transferring them on to a knitting needle. It is also used to make a chain for the lion cub's tail and the vines that cover the arched gateway to the safari park. I use a 3mm (UK 11), the type popular for Amigurumi, but the larger hook is fine and may be more commonly available.

A needle to sew work together Your animals will be sewn together with the yarn you used to knit them. You may usually use a darning needle to sew up your knitted garments, but for this project I recommend a chenille or tapestry needle with a fairly sharp point. Your animal pieces are tightly knitted and you will find it difficult to sew them up with a blunt-ended needle. You can use the same needle for embroidering faces and body parts.

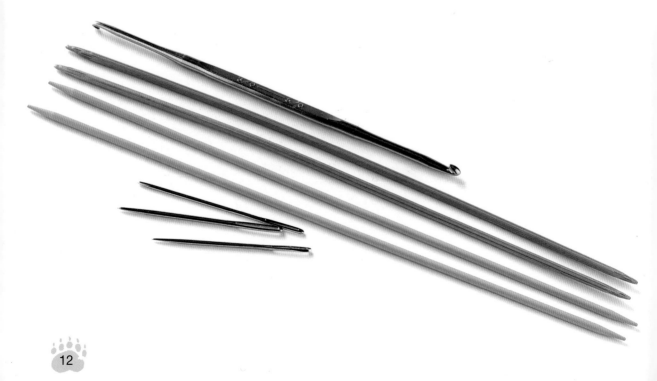

Other materials

Wooden chopsticks This is the best tool to help you stuff small toys. Use it to help you push the stuffing into small parts like legs. If you cannot find them, you can use larger knitting needles or the tips of small embroidery scissors.

Craft pliers These are used to make the arched gateway. They are also very useful to help you pull out a sewing needle from thick layers of knitted pieces.

Erasers Used to make the base for the arched gateway.

Small scissors To cut yarn.

Wire To make the arched gateway. Heavy-duty green garden wire is used to make the basic frame, and fine green garden wire is used to keep the heavy wires together. The animals are not wired, but if you want to give more stability and firmness to the giraffe's legs, you can insert heavy-duty garden wire with the green cover stripped off.

Basic knitting

The knitting skills used in this book are just very basic knit and purl. You can turn small amounts of yarn into something really special with these two simple techniques. All the animals are knitted flat with two needles.

To increase one stitch, knit into the front loop and the back loop of the same stitch. This will not create a hole, unlike picking up between the stitches or bringing the yarn forward. To decrease one stitch, knit or purl two stitches together.

Always leave a long end when casting on and fastening off, for sewing up the piece later. Tuck in all the yarn ends without cutting. You can use the ends to stuff the small parts of the animal too; not only can reduce waste in this way, but the colour will match and so the stuffing will not be visible.

I have used only a couple of crochet techniques: making chains and slip stitch (single stitch).

Tension (gauge)

This is a rough guide. But do not worry, it is not essential to follow it, as long as you keep the tension consistent throughout.
12 sts and 16 rows to a 4cm (1½ in) square over st/st on 2.75mm (UK 12/US 2) knitting needles.

Tip

Stretch your hands from time to time: if you are not used to knitting tight pieces with small needles, rest your hands once in a while, then open and close them to prevent them from becoming stiff.

Abbreviations

Knitting

st/st	stocking stitch (knit on right side rows, purl on wrong side rows)
k	knit
p	purl
inc	increase
dec	decrease
k2tog	knit 2 stitches together
p2tog	purl 2 stitches together
kf/b	knit into front and back of stitch (increasing one stitch)
st(s)	stitch(es)
g-st	garter stitch (knit every row)
pf/b	purl into front and back of stitch (increasing one stitch)

Crochet

ch	chain
ss	slip stitch: Insert hook into chain and wrap yarn round hook. Draw a new loop through both the chain and the loop on the hook, ending with one loop on the hook.

Sewing up and stuffing

The body is tightly knitted and the edges curl, which you may find difficult to work with. If so, press the knitted body piece gently with a steam iron, with a cloth between the piece and the iron.

Some knitted pieces are quite small, and you might find it fiddly to sew them up, so take your time. Mattress stitch, overcast stitch and some running stitches are used.

These are the body, ear, tusk and tail pieces for the elephant. The basic instructions for sewing up the body are the same for most of the animals.

1 Start with a hind leg. Thread a needle with the leftover yarn and go in from the wrong side of the knitted body piece.

2 Use running stitch to sew along the base of the hind leg, then pull up the stitches to close the hole at the base of the leg.

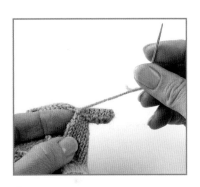

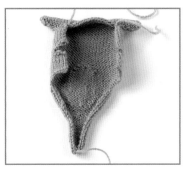

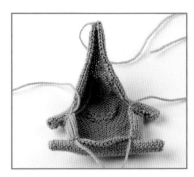

3 Use overcast stitch to sew from the base up the hind leg to close it.

4 Sew the opposite hind leg in the same way. Since there is no leftover yarn here, simply thread the needle with the same coloured yarn.

5 Repeat the same stitching process for the front limbs.

6 Pinch the tail end as shown and use overcast stitch to sew from between the hind legs to the end.

7 Push the needle through to hide the yarn inside the body.

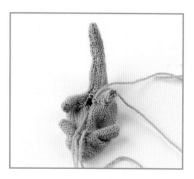

8 Use mattress stitch to sew from the tip of the trunk to between the front legs. Pull the yarn taut to make the trunk bend down.

9 The animal is now ready for stuffing. Take small pieces of stuffing and push them into the extremities with a chopstick or knitting needle.

10 The elephant is now stuffed and ready for sewing up. Sew up the opening with mattress stitch.

11 Fold one of the elephant's ears in half and sew the edges together with mattress stitch.

12 Sew the ear onto the elephant with overcast stitch. Sew on the tusks with matching thread and the tail with body colour thread.

The elephant, sewn up and stuffed.

Basic embroidery

Some simple embroidery stitches are used to complete the animals. I use fine, 2- or 3-ply yarn or two strands taken from DK (8-ply) yarn to embroider faces.

French knots

These are used for most of the animals' eyes. Take the needle through the yarn, separating the fibres, instead of taking the needle out between the stitches. This prevents the eye from sinking into the face.

1 Bring the thread through where the knot is required, at A. Holding the thread between your thumb and finger, wrap it around the needle twice.

2 Hold the thread firmly with your thumb and turn the needle back to A. Insert it as close to A as possible, at B, and pull the thread through to form a knot.

3 Make a small stitch on the wrong side of the fabric before fastening off.

Most of the animals, like this lion, have French knots for eyes.

Back stitch

This is used for the zebra's and tiger's stripes.

1 Bring the needle up at A and pull the thread through. Insert the needle at B and bring it through at C. Pull the thread through the fabric.

2 Insert the needle at D and bring it up at E. Pull the thread through.

3 Insert the needle at F and bring it up at G. Continue working along the stitch line until it is completed. To finish off, thread your needle through the stitches on the wrong side of your work.

The zebra and tiger with their back stitch stripes.

Chain stitch

This is used to create the pattern on the giraffe's coat.

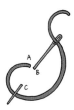  

1 Bring the needle up through the fabric at A and pull the thread through. Insert the needle at B, as close as possible to A, and bring it up at C. Keep the thread under the needle. Pull the thread through gently to form the first chain.

2 Insert the needle at D, as close as possible to C, and bring the needle up at E. Keeping the thread under the needle, pull the thread through gently to form the second chain.

3 Continue in this way, making evenly sized chain stitches, until the line of stitching is complete.

The giraffe with his chain stitch patterned coat.

Decorating the Camper Van

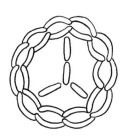 

This is the pattern for the embroidery on the front of the Camper Van.

This is the pattern for the embroidery on the sides and back of the Camper Van.

The Camper Van with its peace symbol at the front and flower embroidery on the back and sides.

Other techniques

How to make an i-cord

I-cords are used for many animal body parts including the gazelle's horns (right) and the elephant's tail. Using double-pointed needles, cast on the required number of stitches. Do not turn. Slide stitches to the opposite end of the needle, then knit stitches again, taking the yarn firmly across the back of the work. Repeat to the desired length. Cast off.

The gazelle, complete with i-cord horns.

Making a mane

1 Cut a piece of card to the size you require. Wind yarn around the card, just as you would to make a tassel. Sew along the centre; you can use a sewing machine if you like.

2 Cut the sides as you would for a tassel.

3 Tear the card away to release the yarn.

The zebra with its mane.

Making a tail

This can be done in one of two ways: you can make an i-cord as above and attach a small tassel on the end, or you can make a twisted skein as follows.

1 Double a length of yarn and knot the ends. Make a fairly long loop and twist it many times with a finger in the loop.

2 Push the loop at one end through the loop at the other end.

3 Allow the skein to form a tight twist. Trim the ends.

The buffalo and giraffe showing off their tails!

Making knitted eyes

Most eyes are simply French knots, but some are made in the following way.

1 Cast on 8 stitches in black yarn. Thread the yarn end on to a tapestry needle, then push the stitches on to the tapestry needle.

2 Pull the needle through, go into the same end of the stitches again and pull through a second time.

3 You should now have a half-circle. Put the needle through the centre and come out at the outer edge. Repeat to create an oval.

The panda has eyes knitted in this way. Simply embroider white French knots to finish.

Adding character

These animal patterns are simple, and some are similar to each other. In the beginning you might think your work doesn't look anything like the animal you are trying to make, but don't despair. You can add a lot of character during the stuffing process. For example, when you are making a large animal like the buffalo, stuff to the hips and the upper body firmly and shape the head triangle by adding stuffing round the neck. To make a gorilla, stuff the upper body firmly to create shoulders, and use less stuffing around the waist. You can use more stuffing for the male lion than the female for stockiness, to differentiate between them. In this way, although they share the same pattern, you can create different looks.

Study the real animal in pictures and note the positions and shapes of their eyes and ears. For instance, if you embroider the eyes in a slightly triangular shape, the animal will look more cat-like.

To complete the elephant, sew a line of running stitch down the underside of the trunk, then pull to gather (see right). The trunk will bend further downwards.

Making small body parts with embroidery

Back stitch on the same spot

This is used to make small body parts such as the monkey's ears, feet and hands, the joey's ears and the penguin's beak. Thread yarn through the needle. Bring the needle to the front of the work. Insert the needle from front to back and repeat. Work on the same spot so that you can build up small body parts with yarn.

Making larger or smaller animals using the same pattern

You can make bigger or smaller animals by adapting the yarn and needle size. You can use Aran yarn or add fine strands, 2- or 3-ply yarn for example, to double knit yarn. I sometimes mix yarn to change the appearance of the work. You can make tiny characters if you use 4-ply yarns.

Go wild and use your imagination

You can be innovative when you are knitting this mini safari scene and try out your own ideas; you do not have to follow all the steps precisely. There's plenty of room for improvisation. For instance, I have modified the pattern so that crochet will not be required to make the safari park, but if you do crochet, you can make the pond on the safari mat with a crochet circle, or make crochet clusters for the rocks round it.

Making the animals

Elephant

Instructions

This is a good project to start with. The pieces are not too small, so it is fairly easy to make. Practise with this pattern. The sewing up method for the other animals is similar.

Body

Cast on 31 sts with grey yarn.
Rows 1–8: st/st, starting with a k row.
Row 9: Cast off 4 sts, k to end (27 sts).
Row 10: Cast off 4 sts, p to end (23).
Row 11: Cast on 4 sts, k to end (27).
Row 12: Cast on 4 sts, p to end (31).
Rows 13–22: st/st, starting with a k row.
Row 23: Cast off 4 sts, k to end (27).
Row 24: Cast off 4 sts, p to end (23).
Row 25: Cast on 4 sts, k these 4 sts, k14, kf/b, k1, kf/b, k to end (29).
Row 26: Cast on 4 sts, p to end (33).
Row 27: k14, (kf/b, k1) twice, kf/b, k14 (36).
Row 28: p.
Row 29: k14, kf/b, k6, kf/b, k14 (38).
Rows 30–32: st/st.
Row 33: Cast off 4, k to end (34).
Row 34: Cast off 4, p to end (30).
Row 35: Cast off 4, k to end (26).
Row 36: Cast off 4, p to end (22).
Row 37: inc 1 st at both ends (24).

Row 38: p.
Row 39: k7, k2tog, k6, k2tog, k7 (22).
Rows 40–42: st/st.
Row 43: k6, k2tog, k6, k2tog, k6 (20).
Row 44: p.
Row 45: (k2tog, k1) 6 times, k2tog (13).
Rows 46–48: st/st.
Row 49: (k2, k2tog) 3 times, k1 (10).
Rows 50–60: st/st.
Row 61: (k2tog, k2) twice, k2tog (7).
Rows 62–63: st/st.
Break yarn, leaving a long end. Draw it through sts on needle, pull up tightly and fasten off.

Ears: make two

Cast on 12 sts with grey yarn.
Row 1: p.
Row 2: k3, kf/b, k4, kf/b, k3 (14).
Row 3: p.
Row 4: k4, kf/b, k4, kf/b, k4 (16).

Materials

DK (8-ply) yarn: 15g (½oz) of grey, small amounts of dark brown or black and small amount of white

Fine 2 or 3-ply yarn: small amount of dark brown (or use 2 strands from DK (8-ply)

Stuffing

Size
12cm (4¾in) long, 6cm (2⅜in) high

Difficulty level
Beginner

Row 5: p.
Row 6: (k4, k2tog) twice, k4 (14).
Row 7: p.
Row 8: k3, k2tog, k4, k2tog, k3 (12).
Row 9: p.
Row 10: (k2tog, k1) (8).
Row 11: p.
Break yarn, draw yarn through sts on needle, pull tightly and fasten off. Fold the piece in half and sew up the sides and cast-on edges.

Tusks: make two

Cast on 4 sts with white yarn.
Rows 1–3: st/st, starting with a k row.
Row 4: p1, p2tog, p1 (3).
Row 5: k.
Row 6: p1, p2tog (2).
Break yarn, draw it through sts on needle, pull up tightly and fasten off. Fold the piece in half and sew up the sides and cast-on edges.

Tail

Cast on 2 sts with grey yarn and make a 2cm (¾in) i-cord. Fasten off. Make a small tassel using fine brown yarn, and attach it to the i-cord.

Making up

After sewing together, as shown on pages 16–17, attach the ears, tusks and tail to the body. Embroider French knots in black or dark brown yarn for the eyes.

Brown Bear

Instructions

Adult body

Cast on 25 sts with brown yarn.
Rows 1–6: st/st, starting with a k row.
Row 7: Cast off 3 sts, k to end (22 sts).
Row 8: Cast off 3 sts, p to end (19).
Row 9: Cast on 3 sts, k to end (22).
Row 10: Cast on 3 sts, p to end (25).
Rows 11–18: st/st.
Row 19: Cast off 3 sts, k to end (22).
Row 20: Cast off 3 sts, p to end (19).
Row 21: Cast on 3 sts, k these 3 sts, k11, kf/b, k1, kf/b, k to end (24).
Row 22: Cast on 3 sts, p to end (27).
Row 23: k12, kf/b, k1, kf/b, k to end (29).
Row 24: p.
Row 25: k13, kf/b, k1, kf/b, k to end (31).
Row 26: p.
Row 27: Cast off 3 sts, k to end (28).
Row 28: Cast off 3 sts, p to end (25).
Row 29: Cast off 6 sts, k to end (19).
Row 30: Cast off 6 sts, p to end (13).
Row 31: (k1, k2tog) to last st, k1 (9).
Row 32: p.
Break yarn, draw yarn through sts on needle, pull tightly and fasten off.

Ears: make two

Cast on 6 sts with brown yarn. Break yarn, draw yarn through sts on needle, pull tightly and fasten off. Follow page 21, steps 1 and 2, to make the ear into a half-circle.

Tail

Cast on 6 sts with brown yarn. Break yarn, draw it through sts on needle, pull tightly and fasten off.

Making up

Sew up as shown on pages 16–17. Attach the ears and tail to the body. Embroider the eyes, nose and mouth with dark brown yarn as shown.

Bear cub

Body

Cast on 15 sts with brown yarn.
Rows 1–4: st/st, starting with a k row.
Row 5: Cast off 2 sts, k to end (13 sts).
Row 6: Cast off 2 sts, p to end (11).
Row 7: inc 1 st at both ends (13).
Rows 8–11 st/st.
Row 12: dec 1 st at both ends (11).
Row 13: Cast on 2 sts, k these 2 sts, k6, kf/b, k1, kf/b, k to end (15).
Row 14: Cast on 2 sts, p to end (17).
Row 15: k7, kf/b, k1, kf/b, k to end (19).
Row 16: p.

Materials

To make one adult and two cubs:

DK (8-ply) yarn: 15g (½oz) of brown and a small amount of dark brown

Stuffing

Sizes

Adult: 7cm (2¾in) long, 5cm (2in) high

Cub: 5cm (2in) long, 3cm (1¼in) high

Difficulty level

Adult: beginner

Cub: intermediate

Row 17: Cast off 4 sts, k to end (15).
Row 18: Cast off 4 sts, p to end (11).
Row 19: dec 1 st at both ends (9).
Row 20: p.
Row 21: (k1, k2tog) to end (6).
Row 22: p.
Row 23: k2tog, k2, k2tog (4).
Row 24: p.
Break yarn, draw yarn through sts on needle, pull tightly and fasten off.

Ears: make two

Cast on 3 sts with brown yarn. Break yarn, draw yarn through sts on needle, pull tightly and fasten off. Follow page 21, steps 1 and 2, to make the ear into a half-circle.

Making up

Sew the body, as shown on pages 16–17, except that when you sew the front legs, sew the length of two stitches from the tip to make each leg. Attach ears to the body. Embroider the eyes, nose and mouth with dark brown yarn. Make a French knot for the tail with brown yarn.

Polar Bear

Instructions

Adult body

Cast on 27 sts with white yarn.
Rows 1–7: st/st, starting with a k row.
Row 8: Cast off 3 sts, p to end (24).
Row 9: Cast off 3 sts, k to end (21).
Row 10: Cast on 3 sts, p to end (24).
Row 11: Cast on 3 sts, k to end (27).
Rows 12–19: st/st.
Row 20: Cast off 3 sts, p to end (24).
Row 21: Cast off 3 sts, k to end (21).
Row 22: Cast on 3 sts, p to end (24).
Row 23: Cast on 3 sts, k these 3 sts, k12, kf/b, k1, kf/b, k to end (29).
Row 24: p.
Row 25: k13, kf/b, k1, kf/b, k to end (31).
Row 26: p.
Row 27: k14, kf/b, k1, kf/b, k to end (33).
Row 28: p.
Row 29: k15, kf/b, k1, kf/b, k to end (35).
Row 30: p.
Row 31: k11, (kf/b, k11) to end (37).
Row 32: Cast off 3 sts, p to end (34).
Row 33: Cast off 3 sts, k to end (31).
Row 34: Cast off 7 sts, p to end (24).
Row 35: Cast off 7 sts, k to end (17).

Row 36: p.
Row 37: (k2tog, k1) to last 2 sts, k2tog (11).
Row 38: p.
Row 39: k2tog, k to last 2 sts, k2tog (9).
Row 40: p.
Break yarn, draw yarn through sts on needle, pull tightly and fasten off.

Ears: make two

Cast on 6 sts with white yarn. Break yarn, draw yarn through sts on needle, pull tightly and fasten off. Follow page 21, steps 1 and 2, to make the ear into a half-circle.

Tail

Cast on 8 sts with white yarn. Break yarn, draw it through sts on needle, pull tightly to make a ball.

Making up

Sew up as shown on pages 16–17. Stuff the shoulders and bottom firmly to add character. Close the seam. Attach the ears and tail. Embroider the eyes, nose and mouth with dark brown yarn as shown.

Materials

To make one adult and two cubs:

DK (8-ply) yarn: 20g (¾oz) of white and a small amount of dark brown

Stuffing

Sizes

Adult: 7cm (2¾in) long, 5cm (2in) high

Cub: 5cm (2in) long, 3cm (1¼in) high

Difficulty level

Mother: beginner

Cub: intermediate

Polar bear cub

Same as the brown bear cub, but with white yarn.

30

Hippopotamus

Instructions

Body

Cast on 25 sts with light brown yarn.

Rows 1–6: st/st, starting with a k row.

Row 7: Cast off 3 sts, k to end (22).

Row 8: Cast off 3 sts, p to end (19).

Row 9: Cast on 3 sts, k to end (22).

Row 10: Cast on 3 sts, p to end (25).

Rows 11–18: st/st, starting with k row.

Row 19: Cast off 3 sts, k to end (22).

Row 20: Cast off 3 sts, p to end (19).

Row 21: Cast on 3 sts, k these 3 sts, k11, kf/b, k1, kf/b, k to end (24).

Row 22: Cast on 3 sts, p to end (27).

Row 23: k10, (kf/b, k1) 3 times, kf/b, k to end (31).

Row 24: p.

Row 25: k11, kf/b, k7, kf/b, k to end (33).

Row 26: p.

Row 27: Cast off 3 sts, k to end (30).

Row 28: Cast off 3 sts, p to end (27).

Row 29: Cast off 6 sts, k to end (21).

Row 30: Cast off 6 sts, p to end (15).

Row 31: inc 1 st at both ends (17).

Rows 32–34: st/st.

Row 35: k4, k2tog, k5, k2tog, k4 (15).

Row 36: Cast off 3 sts, p to end (12).

Row 37: Cast off 3 sts, k to end (9).

Rows 38–39: st/st.

Cast off.

Ears: make two

Cast on 2 sts with light brown yarn and k1 row. Pass the first stitch over the second and fasten off.

Tail

Make a 2-stitch i-cord with light brown yarn, for 5 rows. Fasten off.

Eyes: make two

Cast on 6 sts with light brown yarn. Break yarn, draw yarn through sts on needle, pull tightly and fasten off. Follow page 21, steps 1 and 2, to make the ear into a half-circle.

Making up

Sew the hind legs and the front legs, following the sewing instructions on page 17. To make the head, sew the underside of the upper body from where the front legs meet. Sew half-way.

Materials

DK (8-ply) yarn:10g ($^1/_3$oz) of light brown and small amounts of dark brown and black

Stuffing

Size

8cm (3$^1/_8$in) long, 4cm (1½in) high

Difficulty level

Beginner

Using the yarn left at the cast-off end, sew the chin from one corner to the other. The seam should be T-shaped. Stuff the body and close the seam. Stuff the belly and bottom more firmly. Attach the ears, eyes and tail to the body. Embroider the eyes with French knots in black and the nostrils, as shown (right), with dark brown.

Rhinoceros

Instructions

Body

Same as Hippopotamus, but using grey yarn, until row 35.

Row 36: p.

Row 37: k4, k2tog, k3, k2tog, k4 (13).

Rows 38–40: st/st.

Row 41: k3, k2tog, k3, k2tog, k3 (11).

Row 42: p.

Row 43: (k1, k2tog) to last 2 sts, k2tog (7).

Break yarn, draw yarn through sts on needle, pull tightly and fasten off.

Ears and tail

Same as Hippopotamus, but using grey yarn.

Horns

Large: Cast on 4 sts with pale grey yarn.

Rows 1–3: st/st, starting with knit row.

Row 4: p1, p2tog, p1 (3).

Row 5: k.

Row 6: p1, p2tog (2).

Row 7: k2tog and fasten off.

Small: Cast on 3 sts with white yarn.

Row 1: k.

Row 2: p2tog, p1 (2).

Row 3: k2tog and fasten off.

Making up

Sew the body, as shown on pages 16–17. Attach the horns and ears to the head. Embroider the eyes as for the Brown Bear and embroider the mouth in back stitch, using dark brown yarn. Attach the tail.

Materials

DK (8-ply) yarn: 10g ($^1/_3$oz) of grey and small amounts of pale grey and dark brown

Stuffing

Size

10cm (4in) long, 4cm (1½in) high

Difficulty level

Intermediate

Buffalo

Instructions

Body

Cast on 25 sts with dark brown.
Rows 1–6: st/st, starting with a
k row.
Row 7: Cast off 3 sts, k to
end (22).
Row 8: Cast off 3 sts, p to
end (19).
Row 9: Cast on 2 sts, k to
end (21).
Row 10: Cast on 2 sts, p to
end (23).
Rows 11–18: st/st.
Row 19: Cast off 2 sts, k to
end (21).
Row 20: Cast off 2 sts, p to
end (19).
Row 21: Cast on 3 sts, k11, kf/b,
k1, kf/b, k to end (24).
Row 22: Cast on 3 sts, p to
end (27).
Row 23: k4, kf/b, k7, kf/b, k1,
kf/b, k7, kf/b, k4 (31).
Row 24: p.
Rows 25–28: st/st.
Row 29: Cast off 3 sts, k to
end (28).
Row 30: Cast off 3 sts, p to
end (25).
Row 31: Cast off 7 sts, k to
end (18).
Row 32: Cast off 7 sts, p to
end (11).
Row 33: Cast on 3 sts, k to
end (14).
Row 34: Cast on 3 sts, p to
end (17).
Rows 35–37: st/st.
Row 38: p2tog, cast off the stitch
on the right needle, cast off all the
stitches until the last 2 stitches,
p2tog. Pass the first stitch over the
second stitch and fasten off.

Ears: make two

Cast on 2 sts with dark brown
yarn and k 1 row. Pass the first st
over the second st, fasten off.

Tail

Make a twisted skein tail with dark
brown yarn as shown on page 20.

Horns: make two

Cast on 2 sts with grey.
Row 1: k.
Row 2: p.
Row 3: kf/b, k1 (3).
Row 4: p.
Row 5: k1, kf/b, k1 (4).
Row 6: p.
Row 7: k1, kf/b, kf/b, k1 (6).
Rows 8–12: st/st.
Row 13: k1, k2tog twice, k1 (4).
Row 14: p.
Row 15: k1, k2tog, k1 (3).
Row 16: p.
Row 17: k2tog, k1 (2).

Materials

DK (8-ply) yarn: 10g (1/3oz)
of dark brown and small
amounts of grey and white

Stuffing

Size

9cm (3½in) long, 6cm
(2³/8in) high

Difficulty level

Intermediate

Row 18: p.
Pass the first stitch over the
second stitch and fasten off.

To make up

Sew the legs, following the
instructions on pages 16–17.
Starting between the front legs,
sew the underside of the front
body, chin and face. Attach ears
and tail. Sew the seam of each
horn from the tip and attach to
the body. Embroider the eyes with
French knots in white yarn.

Lion

Instructions

Lion

With sand colour, cast on 23 sts.
Rows 1–6: st/st, starting with a k row.
Row 7: Cast off 3 sts, k to end (20).
Row 8: Cast off 3 sts, p to end (17).
Row 9: Cast on 3 sts, k to end (20).
Row 10: Cast on 3 sts, p to end (23).
Rows 11–16: st/st.
Row 17: Cast off 3 sts, k to end (20).
Row 18: Cast off 3 sts, p to end (17).
Row 19: Cast on 3 sts, k these 3 sts, k10, kf/b, k1, kf/b, k to end (22).
Row 20: Cast on 3 sts, p to end (25).
Row 21: k11, kf/b, k1, kf/b, k to end (27).
Row 22: p.
Row 23: k12, kf/b, k1, kf/b, k to end (29).
Row 24: p.
Row 25: Cast off 3 sts, k to end (26).
Row 26: Cast off 3 sts, p to end (23).
Row 27: Cast off 4 sts, k to end (19).
Row 28: Cast off 4 sts, p to end (15).
Rows 29–30: st/st.
Row 31: k4, k2tog, k3, k2tog, k to end (13).
Row 32: p.
Row 33: (k3, k2tog) twice, k to end (11).
Row 34: p.
Row 35: k3, k2tog, k1, k2tog, k to end (9).
Row 36: p.
Break yarn, draw it through sts on needle, pull tightly and fasten off.

Ears: make two

With sand colour yarn, cast on 2 sts and k 1 row. Pass the first st over the second st and fasten off.

Tail

Make a 2-stitch i-cord with sand colour yarn, for 4 rows. Make a small tassel with fine dark brown yarn, and attach to the cord.

Mane

Make a 9 x 2cm (3½ x ¾in) mane with dark brown yarn, following the technique on page 20.

Making up

Sew the legs, following the instructions on pages 16–17. Starting between the front legs, sew the underside of the front body, chin and face. Attach the mane and the tail. Embroider the eyes with short back stitches and pull the thread gently to make a slight dent in the face. Embroider the nose and mouth as shown.

Lioness

For the body and ears, follow the Lion pattern.

Tail

Make a 2-stitch i-cord for 12 rows. Fasten off.

Making up

As for the Lion, without a mane.

Materials

To make a lion, lioness and two cubs:

DK (8-ply) yarn: 15g (½oz) sand colour and small amounts of black and dark brown

Fine 2 or 3-ply yarn: small amount of dark brown

Stuffing

Extra equipment

3.25mm (UK 10/US D) crochet hook

Sizes

Adult: 8cm (3⅛in) long, 5cm (2in) high

Cub: 4.5cm (1¾in) long, 3cm (1¼in) high

Difficulty level

Intermediate

Cub

Cast on 15 sts with sand colour yarn.
Rows 1–3: st/st, starting with k row.
Row 4: Cast off 2 sts, p to end (13).
Row 5: Cast off 2 sts, k to end (11).
Row 6: inc 1 st at both ends (13).
Row 7: k.
Row 8: p.
Row 9: dec 1 st at both ends (11).
Row 10: Cast on 2 sts, p to end (13.)
Row 11: Cast on 2 sts, k these 2 sts, k6, kf/b k1, kf/b, k to end (17).
Row 12: p.
Row 13: k7, kf/b, k1, kf/b, k to end (19).

Row 14: Cast off 5 sts, p to end (14).

Row 15: Cast off 5 sts, k to end (9).

Row 16: p.

Row 17: k.

Row 18: p2, p2tog, p1, p2tog, p2 (7).

Row 19: k.

Break yarn, draw it through sts on needle, pull tightly and fasten off.

Tail

Make 6 chains in sand colour yarn with a crochet hook and fasten off.

Making up

As for the Lioness, but when you sew the front legs, sew the length of 3 stitches from the tip. Create ears by back stitching in the same place a few times with sand colour yarn. Attach the tail and embroider the eyes, nose and mouth, as for the Lioness.

Tiger

Instructions

Tigress

For the body and ears, with yellow yarn, follow the Lioness pattern.

Tail

Make 2-stitch i-cord for 12 rows. Fasten off. Embroider stripes with black yarn.

Making up

Sewing method is the same as for the Lioness. Embroider stripes with black yarn.

Materials

To make a tigress and two cubs:

DK (8-ply) yarn: 15g (½oz) of yellow and a small amount of black

Stuffing

Sizes

Adult: 8cm (3⅛in) long, 5cm (2in) high

Cub: 4.5cm (1¾in) long, 3cm (1¼in) high

Difficulty level

Intermediate

Cub

With yellow yarn, follow the lion cub pattern.

Tail

Make 2-stich i-cord with yellow yarn for 10 rows. Fasten off. Embroider stripes with black yarn.

Alternatives

You can make a spotted leopard by following the lioness pattern and embroidering spots with black yarn, or a black leopard by knitting with black yarn.

Tapir

Instructions

Adult

Cast on 23 sts with warm grey yarn.

Rows 1–6: st/st, starting with a k row.

Row 7: Cast off 3 sts, k to end (20).

Row 8: Cast off 3 sts, p to end (17).

Row 9: Cast on 2 sts, k to end (19).

Row 10: Cast on 2 sts, p to end (21).

Rows 11–16: st/st.

Row 17: Cast off 2 sts, k to end (19).

Row 18: Cast off 2 sts, p to end (17).

Row 19: Cast on 3 sts, k to end (20).

Row 20: Cast on 3 sts, p to end (23).

Rows 21–26: st/st.

Row 27: Cast off 3 sts, k to end (20).

Row 28: Cast off 3 sts, p to end (17).

Row 29: Cast off 2 sts, k to end (15).

Row 30: Cast off 2 sts, p to end (13).

Row 31: k5, k2tog, k6 (12).

Row 32: p.

Row 33: k5, k2tog, k5 (11).

Row 34: p.

Row 35: k4, k2tog, k5 (10).

Row 36: p.

Row 37: k4, k2tog, k4 (9).

Row 38: p.

Row 39: k3, k2tog, k4 (8).

Rows 40–42: st/st.

Break yarn, draw yarn through sts on needle, pull tightly and fasten off.

Ears: make two

Cast on 2 sts with warm grey yarn and k1 row. Pass the first st over the second st and fasten off.

Making up

Follow the instructions on pages 16–17. Attach the ears and embroider the eyes with French knots in black yarn.

Malayan (two-colour) Tapir

Follow the Tapir pattern, except st/st rows 1–7 with dark grey. At row 8, after casting off 3 stitches with dark grey, join in white and st/st up to row 18 with white. At row 19, join dark grey and cast on 3 sts with dark grey. St/st with dark grey all the way to the end.

Ears: make two

Same as Tapir, but with dark grey yarn.

Calf

Cast on 14 sts with brown yarn.

Rows 1–4: st/st, starting with a k row.

Row 5: Cast off 2 sts, k to end (12).

Row 6: Cast off 2 sts, p to end (10).

Row 7: Cast on 2 sts, k to end (12).

Row 8: Cast on 2 sts, p to end (14).

Rows 9–10: st/st.

Row 11: Cast off 2 sts, k to end (12).

Row 12: Cast off 2 sts, p to end (10).

Materials

To make an adult and calf:

DK (8-ply) yarn: 5g (¹/₆oz) of warm grey and small amounts of brown, beige and black

Stuffing

For the Malayan Tapir:

DK (8-ply) yarn: 5g (¹/₆oz) each of white and dark grey

Stuffing

Sizes

Adult: 9cm long, 4cm high

Calf: 4cm long, 3cm high

Difficulty level

Adult: beginner

Calf: intermediate

Row 13: Cast on 2 sts, k to end (12).

Row 14: Cast on 2 sts, p to end (14).

Rows 15–16: st/st.

Row 17: Cast off 3 sts, k to end (11).

Row 18: Cast off 3 sts, p to end (8).

Row 19: k3, ktog, k3 (7).

Row 20: p.

Row 21: k2, k2tog, k3 (6).

Row 22: p.

Row 23: k2tog to end (3).

Row 24: p.

Break yarn, draw yarn through sts on needle, pull tightly and fasten off.

Making up

Sew the body, following the usual instructions on page 16–17. Back stitch on the same spot two to three times with body colour yarn to create ears. Embroider the eyes with French knots in black yarn and the stripes with back stitch in beige yarn.

Zebra

Instructions

Body

Cast on 24 sts with white yarn.
Rows 1–6: st/st, starting with
k row.
Row 7: Cast off 6 sts, k to end (18).
Row 8: Cast off 6 sts, p to end (12).
Row 9: Cast on 3 sts, k to end (15).
Row10: Cast on 3 sts, p to
end (18).
Rows 11–18: st/st.
Row 19: Cast off 3 sts, k to
end (15).
Row 20: Cast off 3 sts, p to
end (12).
Row 21: Cast on 6 sts, k these 6
sts, k11, kf/b twice, k to end (20).
Row 22: Cast on 6 sts, p to
end (26).
Row 23: k12, kf/b twice, k to
end (28).
Row 24: p.
Row 25: k13, kf/b twice, k to
end (30).
Row 26: p.
Row 27: Cast off 6 sts, k to
end (24).
Row 28: Cast off 6 sts, p to
end (18).
Row 29: Cast off 4 sts, k to
end (14).
Row 30: Cast off 4 sts, p to
end (10).
Row 31: Cast on 3 sts, k to
end (13).
Row 32: Cast on 3 sts, p to
end (16).
Row 33: k.
Row 34: p.
Row 35: k2tog, cast off the stitch
on the right needle, cast off all the
stitches until the last 2 stitches,
k2tog, pass the first stitch over the
second stitch and fasten off.

Ears: make two

Cast on 2sts with white yarn and
k 1 row. Pass the first st over the
second st and fasten off.

Tail

Make a tail with dark brown
yarn, following the technique
on page 20.

Mane

Make a 1.5 x 5cm (½ x 2in)
mane with dark brown yarn,
following the technique
on page 20.

Making up

Sew the legs, following the
instructions on pages 16–17.
Starting between the front legs,
sew the underside of the front
body, chin and face. Attach the
ears, mane and tail to the body.
Embroider the stripes and eyes in
back stitch using black yarn.

Materials

DK (8-ply) yarn: 7g (¼oz) of
white and a small amount
of black

Fine 2 or 3-ply yarn: a small
amount of dark brown

Stuffing

Size

7cm (2¾in) long, 5cm (2in) high

Difficultly level

Intermediate

Impala

Instructions

Male

Body

Cast on 24 sts with light brown yarn.

Rows 1–6: st/st, starting with a k row.

Row 7: Cast off 6 sts, k to end (18).

Row 8: Cast off 6 sts, p to end (12).

Row 9: Cast on 3 sts, k to end (15).

Row 10: Cast on 3 sts, p to end (18).

Rows 11–16: st/st.

Row 17: Cast off 3 sts, k to end (15).

Row 18: Cast off 3 sts, p to end (12).

Row 19: Cast on 6 sts, k these 6 sts, k11, kf/b twice, k to end (20).

Row 20: Cast on 6 sts, p to end (26).

Row 21: k12, kf/b twice, k to end (28).

Row 22: p.

Row 23: k13, kf/b twice, k to end (30).

Row 24: p.

Row 25: Cast off 6 sts, k to end (24).

Row 26: Cast off 6 sts, p to end (18).

Row 27: Cast off 4 sts, k to end (14).

Row 28: Cast off 4 sts, p to end (10).

Row 29: k.

Row 30: dec 1 st at both ends (8).

Row 31: Cast on 3 sts, k to end (11).

Row 32: Cast on 3 sts, p to end (14).

Row 33: inc 1 st at both ends (16).

Row 34: p.

Row 35: k2tog, cast off the stitch on the right needle, cast off all the stitches until the last 2 sts, k2tog, pass the first stitch over the second stitch and fasten off.

Ears: make two

Same as the zebra, but with light brown yarn.

Tail

Make a 2-stitch i-cord with light brown yarn for 3 rows. Fasten off.

Antlers: make two

Make a 2-stitch i-cord with dark brown yarn for 8 rows. Leaving a long end, fasten off tightly. From the tip, run the thread through the cord for 1cm (³/₈in), take it out once, put it back in the i-cord, run it through 5mm (¼in), take it out again and back through the i-cord to the end (see diagrams below). Pull gently to make the cord into a double L shape.

Materials

DK (8-ply) yarn: 10g (¹/₃oz) of light brown and a small amount of dark brown
Stuffing

Size

8cm (3¹/₈in) long, 5cm (2in) high

Difficulty level

Intermediate

Making up

Sew the legs, following the instructions on pages 16–17. Starting between the front legs, sew the underside of the front body, chin and face. Work a gathering thread through the stitches at the back of the neck and pull to keep the head up and create a curved neck line. Place the needle back in where it came out and bring it out through the belly (see diagrams below). Pull tightly and secure. Attach ears, tail and antlers. Embroider the eyes and nose with dark brown, as for the Brown Bear.

Female

Make as for the male, but with no antlers and with bigger ears.

Ears: make 2

Cast on 3 sts.
Rows 1–2: st/st, starting with a k row.
Row 3: k1, k2tog (2).
Pass the first st over the second st and fasten off.

Gazelle

Body

The basic pattern is the same as the Impala, but knitted with a coloured pattern.

Cast on 24 sts with light brown yarn.

Rows 1–6: st/st, starting with a knit row.

Row 7: Cast off 6 sts, k to end (18).

Row 8: Cast off 6 sts, p to end (12).

Join in black and white yarns.

Row 9: Cast on 3 sts with white, k these 3 sts, k6 (white), k1 (black), k4 light (brown), k1 (black), k3 (white) (15).

Row 10: Cast on 3 sts with white, p these 3 sts, p2 (white), p1 (black), p6 (light brown), p1 (black), p5 (white) (18).

Row 11: k5 (white), k1 (black), k6 (light brown), k1 (black), k5 (light brown).

Row 12: Keeping the colour pattern correct, p.

Row 13: k4 (white), k1 (black), k8 (light brown), k1 (black), k4 (white).

Row 14: Keeping the colour pattern correct, k.

Row 15: Repeat row 13.

Row16: Repeat row 14.

Row 17: Keeping the colour pattern correct, cast off 3 sts, k to end (15).

Row 18: Keeping the colour pattern correct, cast off 3 sts, p to end (12).

Break off black and white yarns. Work with light brown only.

Row 19: Cast on 6 sts, k5, (kf/b) twice, k to end (20).

Row 20: Cast on 6 sts, p to end (26).

Row 21: k12, (kf/b) twice, k to end (28).

Row 22: p.

Row 23: k13, (kf/b) twice, k to end (30).

Row 24: p.

Row 25: Cast off 6 sts, k to end (24).

Row 26: Cast off 6 sts, p to end (18).

Row 27: Cast off 4 sts, k to end (14).

Row 28: Cast off 4 sts, p to end (10).

Row 29: dec 1 st at both ends (8).

Row 30: p.

Row 31: Cast on 3 sts, k to end (11).

Row 32: Cast on 3 sts, p to end (14).

Row 33: inc 1 st at both ends (16).

Row 34: p.

Row 35: k2tog, cast off the stitch on the right needle, cast off all the sts until the last 2 sts, k2tog, pass the first stitch over the second stitch. Fasten off.

Ears: make two

Same as zebra, but with light brown yarn.

Antlers: make two

Cast on 2 sts with dark brown yarn and work 6 rows as i-cord.

Next row: Pass the first stitch over the second stitch (1).

Slide the stitch to the right as if making an i-cord, *knit the stitch and slide the stitch to the right again. Repeat from * twice more to make three chains. Fasten off.

Tail

Cast on 2 sts with light brown yarn and work 2 rows as i-cord. Fasten off.

Making up

Sew the legs, following the instructions on pages 16–17. Starting between the front legs, sew the underside of the front body, chin and face. Attach the ears, antlers and tail. Embroider the eyes and nose with dark brown yarn.

Materials

DK (8-ply) yarn: 10g ($\frac{1}{3}$oz) light brown and small amounts of white, black and dark brown

Stuffing

Size

8cm (3$\frac{1}{8}$in) long, 6cm (2$\frac{3}{8}$in) high

Difficulty level

Advanced

Giraffe

Instructions

Body

Cast on 27 sts with yellow yarn.

Row 1: k.

Row 2: Join in white yarn and cast on 6 sts with white, p to end with yellow (33).

Row 3: Cast on 6 sts with white and keeping the colour pattern correct, k to end (39).

Rows 4–5: Keeping the colour pattern correct, st/st, twisting the yarns at the back when you change colours.

Row 6: Cast off 6 sts of white, p to end (33).

Row 7: Cast off 6 sts of white, k to end (27).

Row 8: Cast off 5 sts, p to end (22).

Row 9: Cast off 5 sts, k to end (17).

Row 10: Cast on 3 sts, p to end (20).

Row 11: Cast on 3 sts, k to end (23).

Rows 12–19: st/st.

Row 20: Cast off 3 sts, p to end (20).

Row 21: Cast off 3 sts, k to end (17).

Row 22: Cast on 5 sts, p to end (22).

Row 23: Cast on 5 sts, k these sts, k12, kf/b, k1, kf/b, k to end (29).

Row 24: Join in white yarn. Cast on 6 sts with white, p to end with yellow (35).

Row 25: Join in white yarn from the other end. Cast on 6 sts with white and k6 (white), with yellow k13, kf/b, k1, kf/b, keeping the colour pattern correct k to end (43).

Row 26: Keeping the colour pattern correct, p to end.

Row 27: k6 (white), k14, kf/b, k1, kf/b, k14 (yellow), k6 (white) (45).

Row 28: Keeping colour pattern correct, cast off 6 sts (white), p to end (39).

Row 29: Cast off 6 sts (white) k to end (33).

Row 30: Cast off 8 sts, p to end (25).

Row 31: Cast off 8 sts, k to end (17).

Row 32: Cast off 2 sts, p to end (15).

Row 33: Cast off 2 sts, k to end (13).

Rows 34–44: st/st.

Row 45: k6, k2tog, k5 (12).

Rows 46–49: st/st.

Row 50: Cast on 3 sts, p to end (15).

Row 51: Cast on 3 sts, k to end (18).

Rows 52–53: st/st.

Row 54: p2tog, cast off the stitch on the right needle, cast off all the sts until the last 2 sts, p2tog, pass the first stitch over the second stitch and fasten off.

Ears: make two

Cast on 2 sts with yellow yarn and k 1 row, pass the first st over the second st and fasten off.

Horns: make two

Make 2-stitch i-cord with dark brown yarn for 3 rows. Fasten off tightly.

Mane

Make a 1.5 x 7cm (½ x 2¾in) mane with dark brown yarn, following the instructions on page 20.

Tail

Same as zebra.

Materials

DK (8-ply) yarn: 15g (½oz) of yellow and small amounts of white, brown and dark brown

Fine 2 or 3-ply yarn: small amount of dark brown

Stuffing

Heavy-weight garden wire cut into four 5cm (2in) lengths (optional)

Size

9cm (3½in) long; 12cm (4¾in) high

Difficulty level

Advanced

Making up

There are 2 yarn ends on each leg, use one to sew up and the other to stuff the tip of the leg. Sew the edges together as you push down the yarn, starting from where white meets yellow towards the tip. Starting between the front legs, sew the underside of the front body, chin and face. Stuff the body and close the seam on the belly. Embroider lines of chain stitch around the body using brown yarn. Attach the ears, horns, mane and tail. To keep the neck upright, work a gathering thread through the back of the neck and pull to shape (see Making up diagrams, page 46). Embroider the eyes with French knots in fine dark brown yarn.

Tip

If you find the legs bend too much and you do not intend to use the Giraffe as a toy, you can insert garden wire into the legs. Strip off the green covering and insert the wire from the foot end.

Monkey

Instructions

Body

Cast on 15 sts in brown yarn.

Rows 1–4: st/st, starting with a k row.

Row 5: Cast off 4 sts, k to end (11).

Row 6: Cast off 4 sts, p to end (7).

Row 7: Cast on 3 sts, k to end (10).

Row 8: Cast on 3 sts, p to end (13).

Rows 9–10: st/st.

Row 11: Cast off 3 sts, k to end (10).

Row 12: Cast off 3 sts, p to end (7).

Row 13: Cast on 4 sts, k these 4 sts, k6, kf/b, k1, kf/b, k to end (13).

Row 14: Cast on 4 sts, p to end (17).

Row 15: k7, kf/b k1, kf/b, k to end (19).

Row 16: p.

Row 17: Cast off 6 sts, k to end (13).

Row 18: Cast off 6 sts, p to end (7).

Row 19: (kf/b, k1) 3 times, kf/b (11).

Row 20: p.

Row 21: (k2tog) 5 times, k1 (6).

Row 22: p.

Break yarn, draw it through sts on needle, pull tightly and fasten off.

Eyes: make two

Using fine white yarn or 2 strands taken from DK (8-ply), cast on 5 sts. Break yarn, draw it through sts on needle, pull tightly and fasten off. Following the steps on page 21, make the ear into a circle.

Tail

Make a 2-stitch i-cord with brown yarn for 3cm (1¼in). Fasten off.

Muzzle (optional)

With pale pink yarn, cast on 4 sts, break yarn, draw it through sts on needle, pull tightly and fasten off.

Making up

Sew up the body, following the instructions on pages 16–17. Using pale pink yarn, make ears by back stitching on the same spot a few times. Make hands and feet using the same method. Attach the tail and muzzle. Attach white eyes and embroider a French knot in the centre with black yarn. Embroider the nostrils and mouth with brown yarn.

Materials

DK (8-ply) yarn: small amounts of brown and pale pink

Fine 2 or 3-ply yarn: small amounts of white and black – or take two strands from DK (8-ply)

Stuffing

Extra equipment

Sharp sewing needle, pliers (optional)

Size

5cm (2in) long

Difficulty level

Advanced

Tips

When you embroider the centre of the eyes, use a regular fine sewing needle with a sharp end. If you find it difficult to pull the needle out of the face, use craft pliers to help you. Use different colours for variety. You can make the tail stripy if you like.

Gorilla

Instructions

Body

Cast on 19 sts with grey yarn.

Rows 1–6: st/st, starting with a k row.

Row 7: Cast off 3 sts, k to end (16).

Row 8: Cast off 3 sts, p to end (13).

Row 9: Cast on 2 sts, k to end (15).

Row 10: Cast on 2 sts, p to end (17).

Rows 11–16: st/st.

Row 17: Cast off 2 sts, k to end (15).

Row 18: Cast off 2 sts, p to end (13).

Row 19: Cast on 6 sts, k these 6 sts, k11, kf/b, k1, kf/b, k to end (21).

Row 20: Cast on 6 sts, p to end (27).

Row 21: k11, (kf/b, k1) twice, kf/b, k to end (30).

Row 22: p.

Row 23: k13, kf/b, k2, kf/b, k to end (32).

Row 24: p.

Row 25: Cast off 6 sts, k7, kf/b, k2, kf/b, k to end (28).

Row 26: Cast off 6 sts, p to end (22).

Row 27: Cast off 4 sts, k4, (kf/b, k1, kf/b) twice, k to end (20).

Row 28: Cast off 4 sts, p to end (16).

Rows 29–30: st/st.

Row 31: k6, cast off next 4 sts, k to end (12).

Row 32: p2tog, p to last 2 sts, p2tog (10).

Row 33: k.

Row 34: p2tog, cast off the stitch on the right needle, cast off all the stitches until the last 2 sts, p2tog, pass the first stitch over the second stitch and fasten off.

Making up

Sew up each leg, following the instructions on pages 16–17. Sew the front part of the body and face, starting between the front legs. Close the hole in the face and stuff the body. To add character, stuff well into the forehead, upper body and hips. Work a gathering thread through each stitch around the waist and pull up to shape it.

Create the ears by back stitching on the same spot two to three times with grey yarn. Embroider the eyes with French knots in black yarn, then pull the thread gently to shape the face. Embroider the nostrils with small back stitches in dark brown or black yarn and the mouth with back stitch in black yarn.

Materials

DK (8-ply) yarn: 7g (¼oz) of grey and small amounts of dark brown and black yarn

Stuffing

Size

6cm (2⅜in) long, 5cm (2in) high

Difficulty level

Intermediate

Kangaroo

Instructions

Mother

The body and head are knitted as one piece. The legs and arms are knitted separately.

Body

With sand colour yarn, cast on 3 sts.
Row 1: p.
Row 2: k1, kf/b, k1 (4).
Row 3: p.
Row 4: k1, (kf/b) twice, k1 (6).
Row 5: p.
Row 6: k2, (kf/b) twice, k2 (8).
Row 7: p.
Row 8: k3, (kf/b) twice, k3 (10).
Row 9: p.
Row 10: k4, (kf/b) twice, k4 (12).
Row 11: p.
Row 12: k5, (kf/b) twice, k5 (14).
Rows 13–21: st/st, starting with p row.
Row 22: k6, k2tog, k6 (13).
Row 23: p.
Row 24: k5, k2tog, k6 (12).
Row 25: p.
Row 26: k5, k2tog, k5 (11).
Row 27: p.
Row 28: k4, k2tog, k5 (10).
Row 29: p.
Row 30: Cast on 3 sts, k to end (13).
Row 31: Cast on 3 sts, p to end (16).
Rows 32–33: st/st.
Row 34: k2tog, cast off the stitch on the right needle, cast off all the sts until the last 2 sts, k2tog, pass the first stitch over the second stitch and fasten off.

Legs: make two

With sand colour yarn, cast on 8 sts.
Row 1: p.
Row 2: k3, (kf/b) twice, k3 (10).
Row 3: p.
Row 4: k4, (kf/b) twice, k4 (12).
Rows 5–7: st/st.
Row 8: k2tog to end (6).
Row 9: Cast on 3 sts, p to end (9).
Row 10: Cast on 3 sts, k to end (12).
Row 11: p.
Cast off.
Fold the piece in half lengthwise and sew the edges together. Stuff lightly.

Arms: make two

Make a 3-stitch i-cord with sand colour yarn for 7 rows. Fasten off

Ears: make two

Cast on 2 sts with sand colour yarn. K 1 row. Slip the first stitch over the second stitch and fasten off.

Pouch

Cast on 10 sts with sand colour yarn.
Rows 1–4: st/st, starting with k row.
Row 5: (k2, k2tog) twice, k2 (8).
Row 6: p.
Row 7: k2tog to end (4).
Cast off.

Making up

Body: Using the yarn left from the cast-off edge, sew the head, and body stopping halfway at the tummy. Sew up the body from the tail end as well, leaving a little space for stuffing. Stuff and close

Materials

DK (8-ply) yarn: 10g (1/3oz) of sand colour and small amount of dark brown

Stuffing

Size

7cm (2¾in) high

Difficulty level

Advanced

the seam. Attach the arms, legs and pouch to the body. Attach ears to the head, embroider the eyes and the nose with French knots in dark brown yarn.

Joey

The joey has only half a body and does not have legs.

Body

Make a 3-stitch i-cord with sand colour yarn for 5 rows and create head as follows:
Row 6: Cast on 2 sts, p to end (5).
Row 7: Cast on 2 sts, k to end (7).
Row 8: p.
Row 9: k1, (k2tog, k1) to end (5).
Break yarn, draw it through sts on needle, pull tightly and fasten off. Sew the head seam and lightly stuff the head.

Create ears by back stitching on the same spot two or three times with sand colour yarn. Embroider the eyes and nose with French knots in dark brown. Place the joey in the mother's pouch and secure with a few stitches.

Koala

Instructions

Mother

Body

With light grey yarn, cast on 15 sts.

Follow the Brown Bear Cub pattern (page 28) up to row 12.

Row 13: Cast on 2 sts, k these 2 sts, k4, k2tog, k3, k2tog, k2 (11).

Row 14: Cast on 2 sts, p to end (13).

Rows 15–16: st/st.

Row 17: Cast off 3 sts, k to end (10).

Row 18: Cast off 3 sts p to end (7).

Cast off.

Head

With light grey yarn, cast on 4 sts (leave a long end for sewing).

Row 1: p.

Row 2: Cast on 4 sts, k to end (8).

Row 3: Cast on 4 sts, p to end (12), leave a marker.

Rows 4–6: st/st.

Row 7: (p1, p2tog) to end (8).

Rows 8–9: st/st.

Break yarn, draw it through sts on needle, pull tightly and fasten off.

Ears: make two

With light grey yarn, cast on 6 sts. Join in white yarn and knit 1 row. Break yarn, draw it through sts on needle, pull tightly and fasten off.

Tail

Cast on 4 sts. Break yarn, draw it through sts on needle and pull tightly to make a bobble.

Making up

Sew each leg and the underside of the body. Stuff and close the seam. Sew the head from the fastened-off end, to the marker. Stuff the head and close the back of the head. Attach to the body with the head facing sideways. Attach the ears and tail. Embroider the eyes with French knots in dark brown yarn and the nose with back stitches in brown yarn.

Cub

With light grey yarn, cast on 11 sts.

Rows 1–3: st/st.

Row 4: Cast off 2 sts, p to end (9).

Row 5: Cast off 2 sts, k to end (7).

Row 6: inc 1 st at both ends (9).

Rows 7–9: st/st.

Row 10: dec 1 st at both ends (7).

Row 11: Cast on 2 sts, k these 2 sts, k4, k2tog, k3 (8).

Row 12: Cast on 2 sts, p to end (10).

Rows 13–14: st/st.

Row 15: Cast off 2 sts, k to end (8).

Row 16: Cast off 2 sts, p to end (6).

Cast off.

Head

With light grey yarn, cast on 3 sts (leave a long end for sewing).

Row 1: p.

Row 2: Cast on 2 sts, k to end (5).

Row 3: Cast on 2 sts, p to end (7), leave a marker.

Rows 4–5: st/st.

Row 6: k1, k2tog, k1, k2tog, k1(5).

Row 7: p.

Break yarn, draw it through sts on needle, pull tightly and fasten off.

Materials

DK (8-ply) yarn: 10g (1/3oz) of light grey and small amounts of white, dark brown and brown

Stuffing

Size

Adult 5cm (2in) high

Cub: 3cm (1¼in) high

Difficulty level

Advanced

Ears: make two

Cast on 4 sts with light grey yarn and k 1 row. Break yarn, draw it through sts on needle, pull tightly and fasten off.

Tail

As for Mother.

Making up

Follow the sewing instructions for the Mother. Embroider the centre of the Cub's ears with French knots in white yarn if you wish. Sew the Cub to the back of the Mother.

Panda

Instructions

Body

With black yarn, cast on 25 sts.
Rows1–6: st/st, starting with a k row.
Row 7: Cast off 3 sts, k to end (22).
Row 8: Cast off 3 sts, change to white yarn, p to end (19).
Row 9: Cast on 3 sts, k to end (22).
Row 10: Cast on 3 sts, p to end (25).
Rows 11–16: st/st.
Row 17: Cast off 3 sts, k to end (22).
Row 18: Cast off 3 sts, p to end (19).
Row 19: Change to black yarn. Cast on 3 sts, k these 3 sts, k8, k2tog, k5, k2tog, k to end (20).
Row 20: Cast on 3 sts, p to end (23).
Rows 21–24: st/st.
Row 25: Cast off 3 sts, k to end (20).
Row 26: Cast off 3 sts, p to end (17).
Cast off.

Head

With white yarn, cast on 4 sts (leave a long end for sewing).
Row 1: p.
Row 2: Cast on 3 sts, k to end (7).
Row 3: Cast on 3 sts p to end (10).
Row 4: Cast on 2 sts, k to end (12).
Row 5: Cast on 2 sts, p to end (14), leave a marker.
Row 6: (k3, kf/b) 3 times, k2 (17).
Rows 7–10: st/st.

Row 11: (p2tog) to last st, p1 (9).
Rows 12–13: st/st.
Break yarn, draw it through sts on needle, pull tightly and fasten off.

Ears: make two

With black yarn, cast on 7 sts.
Break yarn, draw it through sts on needle, pull tightly and fasten off.
Following page 21, steps 1 and 2, make each ear into a half-circle.

Eyes: make two

Make the eyes, as shown on page 21, starting with black yarn and adding French knots in white yarn.

Tail

Cast on 10sts with white yarn.
Break yarn, draw it through sts on needle and pull tightly to make a bobble.

Making up

Sew each hind leg from the foot, using overcast stitches. Sew the under-body flaps along the cast-off edge. Sew each front leg from the foot. Stuff the legs and close the belly. Using the yarn left over at the fastened-off end, sew the head up to the marker. Stuff the head and attach it to the body using mattress stitch. Attach the eyes, ears and tail. Embroider the nose with black yarn and the mouth with two strands of dark brown yarn, as shown.

Materials

DK (8-ply) yarn: 5g (¹⁄₆oz) white and 5g (¹⁄₆oz) black and a small amount of dark brown

Stuffing

Size

7cm (2¾in) tall

Difficulty level

Advanced

Meerkats

Instructions

Meerkat

With sand colour yarn, follow the Monkey pattern (page 52), but omit the muzzle. Make knitted eyes with dark grey yarn and embroider the centres with white yarn (see page 21).

Rock

This pattern is only a suggested guideline. You can knit this however you like, in any size. You can increase or decrease at both ends at random. It is worked in garter stitch throughout.

Cast on 20 sts and k 1 row.

Increase 1 st at both ends every other row until there are 26 sts.

K 6 rows.

Decrease at both ends of the next 2 rows (22).

K 6 rows.

Decrease at both ends of the next 2 rows (18).

K 1 row.

Decrease at both ends of every other row until there are 14 sts.

K 4 rows.

Decrease at both ends of the next 2 rows (10).

Cast off.

Making up

Fold the piece vertically and sew the edges. Lightly stuff and close the seam. Attach the Meerkats to the Rock.

Materials

To make three Meerkats:

DK (8-ply) yarn: 10g (⅓oz) of sand colour and small amounts of dark grey and white

Stuffing

To make the Rock:

DK (8-ply) yarn: small amount of sand colour

Stuffing

Sizes

Meerkats: 7cm (2¾in) high

Rock: 6 x 4cm (2⅜ x 1½in)

Difficulty level

Meerkats: advanced

Rock: beginner

Penguin

Instructions

Body

Starting with the base, cast on 6 sts with black yarn.
Row 1: kf/b in every st (12).
Row 2: p.
Row 3: (k1, kf/b) to end (18).
Row 4: k (this is the fold line).
Join in white yarn.
Row 5: k6 (black), k6 (white), k6 (black).
Row 6: Keeping the colour pattern correct, p.
Row 7: Keeping the colour pattern correct, k2tog, k to last 2 sts, k2tog (16).
Row 8: Keeping the colour pattern correct, p.
Row 9: k1, k2tog, k2 (black), k2tog, k2, k2tog, (white), k2, k2tog, k1 (black) (12).
Row 10: Keeping the colour pattern correct, p.
Row 11: Break white, k with black only.
Rows 12–16: st/st.
Row 17: (k1, k2tog) to end (8).
Break yarn leaving a long end, draw it through sts on needle, pull tightly and fasten off.

Wings: make two

Cast on 8 sts with black yarn.
Rows 1–3: st/st, starting with a p row.
Row 4: (k1, k2tog) twice, k2 (6).
Row 5: p.
Row 6: (k1, k2tog) to end (4).
Break yarn, draw it through sts on needle, pull tightly and fasten off.

Making up

Using the yarn left at the cast-on edge, gather thread through every stitch along the base edge of the body, pull tightly and fasten off. Join the side edges from the top of the head using the yarn left at the fastened-off end, stuff and close the seam. Pierce the body at the centre of the base with a threaded needle, take it out at the back of the neck and repeat. Pull gently to flatten the base for stability and fasten off. Attach the wings. Embroider the eyes with French knots in white yarn and the feet with back stitches in yellow yarn. To make a beak, back stitch several times on the same spot with yellow yarn.

Materials
DK (8-ply) yarn: 3g (⅛oz) black and small amounts of white and yellow

Stuffing

Size
3cm (1¼in) high

Difficulty level
Intermediate

Pelican

Instructions

Body

Starting with the base, cast on 6 sts with white yarn.

Row 1: kf/b in every st (12).
Row 2: p.
Row 3: (k1, kf/b) to end (18).
Row 4: k for fold line.
Rows 5–6: st/st, starting with a k row.
Row 7: k2tog, k to last 2 sts, k2tog (16).
Rows 8–12: st/st, starting with a p row.
Row 13: k1 (k2tog, k1) to end (11).
Rows 14–17: st/st, starting with a p row.
Row 18: p1, (p2tog) to end (6).
Rows 19–26: st/st, starting with a k row.
Row 27: k1, kf/b, k2, kf/b, k1 (8).
Rows 28–29: st/st.
Row 30: (p2tog) to end (4).
Break yarn, draw it through sts on needle, pull tightly and fasten off.

Beak

Cast on 10 sts with yellow yarn.
Rows 1–5: st/st, starting with a p row.
Row 6: k1, (k2tog, k1) to end (7).
Row 7: p.
Row 8: k1, (k2tog, k1) to end (5).
Row 9: p.
Break yarn, draw it through sts on needle, pull tightly and fasten off.

Wings: make two

Cast on 10 sts with white yarn.
Rows 1–5: st/st, starting with a p row.

Row 6: k2, (k2tog, k2) to end (8).
Row 7: p.
Row 8: Change to black and k.
Row 9: p.
Row 10: (k1, k2tog) twice, k2 (6).
Row 11: p.
Break yarn, draw it through sts on needle, pull tightly and fasten off.

Feet: make two

Cast on 3 sts with yellow yarn and work garter stitch 3 rows. Cast off.

To make up

Using the yarn left at the cast-on edge, gather through every stitch along the first row of the body and pull tightly. Sew the rest of the base seam and the sides, stopping half way for stuffing. Starting at the fastened-off end, sew the head and neck. The seam will be on the chest side. Stuff the body and close the seam.

Materials

DK (8-ply) yarn: 5g (1/6oz) of white, small amounts of black and yellow

Stuffing

Size

5cm (2in) high

Difficulty level

Intermediate

From the centre of the base piece, pierce the body with a threaded needle and take it out at the back of the neck. Repeat. Pull gently to flatten the base for stability. Squash down the neck and secure it to the body to shape. Attach the beak, feet and the wings. Embroider the eyes with French knots in black.

Toucan

Instructions

Body

Same as Penguin (page 64) up to row 4.
Row 5: k.
Row 6: p.
Row 7: k2tog, k to last 2 sts, k2tog (16).
Row 8: p.
Row 9: (k1, k2tog) to last st, k1 (11).
Row 10: p.
Join in white yarn.
Row 11: k4 (black), k3 (white), k4 (black).
Row 12: p3 (black), p5 (white), p3 (black).
Row 13: k2 (black), k7 (white), k2 (black).
Row 14: p1 (black), p9 (white), p1 (black).
Row 15: Break off black yarn and knit with white only.
Row 16: p.
Row 17: (k1, k2tog) 3 times, k2 (8).
Break yarn, draw it through sts on needle, pull tightly and fasten off.

Beak

With yellow yarn, cast on 8 sts.
Rows 1–3: st/st, starting with p row.
Row 4: k2, (k2tog) twice, k2 (6).
Row 5: p.
Row 6: k2, k2tog, k2 (5).
Row 7: p.
Row 8: k2tog, k1, k2tog (3).
Break yarn, draw it through sts on needle, pull tightly and fasten off.

Tail

Work in g-st.
With black yarn, cast on 3 sts.
Rows 1–2: k.
Row 3: k1, k2tog (2).
Rows 4–5: k.
Pass the first stitch over the second stitch and fasten off.

Wings: make two

With black yarn, cast on 6 sts.
Rows 1–3: st/st, starting with a p row.
Row 4: (k1, k2tog) to end (4).
Row 5: p.
Break yarn, draw it through sts on needle, pull tightly and fasten off.

Making up

Follow the Penguin instructions (page 64) to sew the body. Attach the beak, wings and tail. Embroider the eyes with French knots in black yarn and the feet with back stitches in yellow yarn. Embroider the ends of the beak as shown below.

Materials

DK (8-ply) yarn: 3g (⅛oz) of black and small amounts of white and yellow

Stuffing

Size

3.5cm (1⅜in) high

Difficulty level

Intermediate

Parrot

Instructions

Body

Cast on 5 sts in the colour of your choice.
Row 1: kf/b in every st (10).
Row 2: p.
Row 3: (k1, kf/b) to end (15).
Row 4: k for fold line.
Row 5: k.
Row 6: p.
Row 7: k2tog, k to last 2 sts, k2tog (13).
Row 8: p (change colour if you are making a 3-coloured parrot).
Row 9: k1, (k2tog, k1) to end (9).
Row 10: p.
Row 11: Change colour, k.
Row 12: p.
Row 13: k.
Row 14: p.
Row 15: (k1, k2tog) to end (6).
Break yarn, draw it through sts on needle, pull tightly and fasten off.

Beak

With yellow yarn, cast on 3 sts.
Row 1: p.
Row 2: k1, k2tog. Pass the first st over the second st and fasten off. Hide the fastened-off yarn inside the beak and pull gently so that the beak curves inwards.

Wings: make two

Cast on 6 sts in the colour of your choice.
Rows 1–3: st/st, starting with a p row.
Row 4: k1, k2tog twice, k1 (4).
Row 5: p.
Row 6: (k2tog) twice (2).
Pass the first stitch over the second stitch and fasten off.

Note

For shorter, round wings, omit row 6. Thread stitches through a sewing needle after row 5, pull tightly and fasten off.

Tail

Work in g-st.
With main colour, cast on 3 sts.
Rows 1–2: k.
Row 3: k1, k2tog (2).
Row 4: k.
Pass the first stitch over the second stitch and fasten off.

Materials

DK (8-ply) yarn: 3g (⅛oz) in bright colours of your choice and small amounts of black and yellow

Stuffing

Size

3cm (1¼in) high

Difficulty level

Intermediate

Making up

Sew the body as for the Penguin (page 64). Attach the beak, tail and wings. Embroider the eyes with French knots in black yarn, and the feet with back stitches in yellow yarn or your choice of colour. Sew a few strands of yarn on top of the head for a crest, if desired.

Vulture

Instructions

Body

Starting with the base, cast on 6 sts with brown yarn.
Row 1: kf/b in every st (12).
Row 2: p.
Row 3: (k1, kf/b) to end (18).
Row 4: k for fold line.
Rows 5–6: st/st, starting with k row.
Row 7: k2tog, k to last 2 sts, k2tog (16).
Rows 8–12: st/st, starting with p row.
Row 13: (k1 k2tog) 5 times, k1 (11).
Rows 14–17: st/st, starting with p row.
Row 18: (p2tog) 5 times, p1 (6).
Rows 19–22: Change to pink yarn and st/st, starting with a k row.
Row 23: k1, kf/b, k2, kf/b, k1 (8).
Rows 24–26: st/st, starting with a p row.
Row 27: (k2tog) 4 times (4).
Break yarn, draw it through sts on needle, pull tightly and fasten off.

Beak

Same as Parrot (page 70), with yellow yarn.

Wings: make two

With brown yarn, cast on 10 sts.
Rows 1–5: st/st, starting with p row.
Row 6: (k1, k2tog) 3 times, k1 (7).
Rows 7–9: st/st, starting with p row.
Row 10: (k1, k2tog) twice, k1 (5).
Row 11: p.
Break yarn, draw it through sts on needle, pull tightly and fasten off.

Making up

Using the yarn left at the cast-on edge of the body, gather through every stitch along the first row, pull tightly and fasten off. Sew the bottom seam and the sides, leaving enough space for stuffing. Sew the head and neck with pink yarn. The seam will be at the back. Stuff and close the seam.

Materials

DK (8-ply) yarn: 5g (1/6oz) of brown, small amounts of black, yellow and pink

Stuffing

Size

5cm (2in) high

Difficulty level

Intermediate

Pierce the centre of the base with a threaded needle and take it out from the back of the neck. Repeat. Pull gently to flatten the base for stability. Attach the beak and wings. Embroider the eyes with French knots in black yarn and the feet with back stitches in yellow yarn.

Crocodile

Instructions

The body has upper and underside pieces. The head is continued from the upper body piece. The feet are knitted separately.

Upper body piece

Cast on 5 sts with green yarn.
Row 1: (k1, p1) twice, k1.
Rows 2–4: Repeat row 1.
Row 5: kf/b, p1, k1, p1, kf/b (7).
Row 6: (p1, k1) 3 times, p1.
Row 7: kf/b, (k1, p1) twice, k1, kf/b (9),
Row 8: (k1, p1) 4 times, k1 (9).
Rows 9–12: Repeat row 8.
Row 13: k2tog, (k1, p1) twice, k1, k2tog (7).
Row 14: (p1, k1) 3 times, p1.
Row 15: Repeat row 14.
Row 16: k2tog, p1, k1, p1, k2tog (5).
Rows 17–23: (k1, p1) twice, k1.
Row 24: k1, p1, k2tog, k1 (4).
Row 25: (p1, k1) twice.
Row 26: (k1, p1) twice.
Row 27: Repeat row 25.
Row 28: Repeat row 26.
Row 29: Repeat row 25.
Row 30: p1, k2tog, p1 (3).
Rows 31–35: p1, k1, p1.
Row 36: k1, k2tog (2).
Pass the first stitch over the second stitch and fasten off.

Head

With green yarn, pick up 5 sts from the cast-on edge of the body, cast on a further 3 sts (8).
Row 1: p.
Row 2: Cast on 3 sts, k to end (11).
Row 3: p.

Row 4: k4, kf/b, k1, kf/b, k4 (13).
Rows 5–7: st/st.
Row 8: k4, k2tog, k1, k2tog, k4 (11).
Row 9: p.
Row 10: k4, (k2tog) twice, k3 (9).
Row 11: p.
Row 12: k3, (k2tog) twice, k2 (7).
Rows 13–15: st/st.
Break yarn, draw it through sts on needle, pull tightly and fasten off.

Underside

With cream yarn, cast on 5 sts.
Rows 1–20: st/st, starting with a k row.
Row 21: k1, k2tog, k2 (4).
Rows 22–26: st/st.
Row 27: k1, k2tog, k1 (3).
Row 28: p.
Row 29: k.
Row 30: p1, p2tog (2).
Pass the first stitch over the second stitch and fasten off.

Legs: make four

With green yarn, cast on 5 sts.
Rows 1–4: Work as an i-cord.
Bring yarn to the right side through the back of the work just as for making an i-cord.
Row 5: k2tog, slip the st on the right needle back to the left needle, cast on 2 sts using cable casting on method (see opposite). Cast off 2 sts, knit the first st from the left needle. Now you have 2 sts on each needle. Pass the right st over the next st on the right needle. Pass the st on the right needle back to the left needle, cast on 2 sts, cast off 2 sts. k2tog from

Materials

DK (8-ply) yarn: 5g green and small amounts of cream, white and black

Stuffing

Size

10cm (4in) long

Difficulty level

Advanced

the left needle, slip the right st over the left st, slip the last st to left needle, cast on 2 sts, cast off the remaining 3 sts, leaving a long end. Thread the yarn end through a sewing needle and gather the foot.

Eyes: make two

With green yarn, cast on 5 sts. Break yarn, draw it through sts on needle, pull tightly and fasten off. Following page 21, steps 1 and 2, make each eye into a half-circle.

Making up

Sew the head seam from the tip. Sew the upper body piece and underside together, from the tip of the tail. Stuff the head and body and close the seam. Hide the yarn ends of each leg and attach the legs to the body. Embroider the mouth and teeth as follows: with black yarn, embroider a single straight line across the front of the face. With 2 strands taken from white DK (8-ply) yarn, embroider short vertical lines over the black line. Attach the eyes to the head and embroider a back stitch in black yarn for the iris.

Cable casting on method

Use a pair of knitting needles.

1) Make a slip knot on the left-hand needle.

2) Insert the right-hand needle into the slip knot as if to knit. Wrap and pull through as for a regular knit stitch.

3) Place the newly-made stitch back on the left-hand needle.

Snake

Instructions

Knitting

Make a tight i-cord. The snake curls up by itself.

Cast on 4 sts with orange yarn and work as an i-cord.

Work 2 rows with orange, 1 row with grey. Repeat these rows until the i-cord measures 9cm (3½in).

Next row: k1, (kf/b) twice, k1 (6).

Work 2 more rows. Break yarn, draw it through sts on needle, pull tightly and fasten off.

Making up

Hide all yarn ends inside the body. Embroider the eyes with French knots in black yarn. Shape and secure the position with a few stitches. To make the tongue, thread a sewing needle with red yarn, insert it into the snake's neck and take it out at the mouth (see diagram below, left). Cut the red yarn to the desired length. Thread a needle with the other end of the red yarn, insert it into the body and bring the needle out, hiding the thread end inside (see diagram below, right).

Materials

DK (8-ply) yarn: small amounts of orange, grey, black and red, or colours of your choice

Difficulty level

Beginner

Giant Turtle

Instructions

Adult

Top shell

Cast on 28 sts with green yarn.
Row 1: p.
Row 2: k4, (k2tog, k4) to end (24).
Row 3: p.
Row 4: (k4, k2tog) to end (20).
Row 5: p.
Row 6: (k3, k2tog) to end (16).
Row 7: p.
Row 8: k3, k2tog, (k2, k2tog) twice, k3 (13).
Row 9: p.
Row 10: k3, (k2tog, k3) to end (11).
Break yarn, draw it through sts on needle, pull tightly and fasten off.

Underside

Cast on 24 sts with green yarn.
Row 1: p.
Row 2: (k4, k2tog) to end (20).
Row 3: p.
Row 4: (k3, k2tog) to end (16).
Row 5: p.
Row 6: k3, k2tog (k2, k2tog) twice, k3 (13).
Break yarn, draw it through sts on needle, pull tightly and fasten off.

Legs: make four

Cast on 5 sts with light brown yarn and work 4 rows as an i-cord. Break yarn, draw it through sts on needle, pull tightly and fasten off.

Head and neck

Cast on 5 sts with light brown yarn and work 7 rows as an i-cord.
Next row: k1, (kf/b, k1) to end (7).
Work 2 more rows i-cord.

Break yarn, draw it through sts on needle, pull tightly and fasten off.

Tail

Cast on 4 sts with light brown yarn and work 3 rows as an i-cord. Break yarn, draw it through sts on needle, pull tightly and fasten off.

Making up

The legs do not have seams to sew up since they are i-cords, but they may be a little loose at the edges. To tighten the long edges, work mattress stitch. From the fastened-off end of the neck and head, use mattress stitch to sew along the edges to tighten them and pull gently to make the head bend down. Sew up the seams of the shell and underside from the fastened-off end to make a circle of each. Let the shell curl up a little at the edges. Place the shell on the underside, wrong sides facing, meeting at the seams. Place the tail between the shell and underside and sew them together at this point, piercing through the tail to attach it. Join a sewing thread at the front of the shell, sandwich the head piece between the shell and underside and sew together here as well. Attach shell and underside by simply taking out the needle to both ends. When you come to the position of a leg, place it between the shell and underside, tuck in all the yarn ends and continue, sewing all the way round. If you need to add more stuffing, push some in before you close the seam. Run a thread from the bottom centre to the top of the

Materials

To make one adult and one baby:

DK (8-ply) yarn: small amounts of light brown in two shades, green in two shades, black and dark brown

Stuffing

Size

Adult 6cm (2³⁄₈in), baby 4cm (1½in)

Difficulty level

Intermediate

shell and pull to make a dent in the bottom centre. Embroider French knots in black yarn for the eyes.

Baby

Shell

Top and bottom are knitted as one piece, unlike the Adult.
Starting with the base, cast on 7 sts with green yarn.
Row 1: kf/b in each st (14).
Row 2: p.
Row 3: (k1, kf/b) to end (21).
Row 4: k for fold line.
Rows 5–9: st/st, starting with k row.
Row 10: p1, (p1, p2tog, p1) to end (16).
Row 11: (k2tog) to end (8).
Break yarn, draw it through sts on needle, pull tightly and fasten off.

Head and neck

Cast on 4 sts with light brown yarn and work 5 rows as an i-cord.

Next row: Shape neck, k1, (kf/b) twice, k1 (6).

Break yarn, draw it through sts on needle, pull tightly and fasten off.

Making up

Using the yarn left at the fastened-off end, sew the top shell seam. Using the yarn left at the cast-on edge, gather through every stitch along the first row and draw up tightly. Stuff the body and close the base seam. At the centre of the base, pierce the body with a threaded needle and take it out from the centre of the top shell twice, pulling gently to flatten the base. Create legs by back stitching on the spot three times with light brown yarn. Make up the neck as for the Adult and attach. Embroider French knots for eyes in dark brown or black yarn.

Safari Mat

Instructions

The mat is a patchwork of many knitted squares. It is a very relaxed project. You can make squares of any size, with any yarn. You can experiment with new stitch patterns. This project also gives a good opportunity for beginners to practise knitting. If you use stocking stitch all the way from the beginning to end, the sides will curl up. Use garter stitch or moss stitch on the four sides. Knit and keep making squares. You can change colours or stitch patterns without breaking the yarn. When you think you have made about 70% of the mat, press the squares with an iron, then arrange and sew them together. See how many more you need, in what size, and make more squares to fill in the space. Here are some suggestions for squares.

Square A

Cast on 22 sts, knit every row (garter stitch) until the work measures 6cm (2⅜in). Cast off.

Square B

Cast on 22 sts, k 1 row.
Next row: k3, (k1, p1) to last 3 sts, k3.
Rep this row until the work measures 6cm (2⅜in) and k 1 row. Cast off.

Square C

Cast on 25 sts, and k 2 rows.
Row 1: (k5, p5) twice, k5.
Row 2: (p5, k5) twice, p5.
Rows 3 and 5: same as row 1.
Rows 4 and 6: same as row 2.
Row 7: (p5, k5) twice, p5.

Row 8: (k5, p5) twice, k5.
Row 9 and 11: same as row 7.
Rows 10 and 12: same as row 8.
Repeat rows 1–12 twice more.
Cast off.

Square D

Cast on 21 sts.
Row 1: k.
Row 2: k2, p17, k2.
Repeat the last 2 rows until the work measures 5cm (2in) and k 1 row.

Pond

You can make a pond with a crochet circle if you like, but I made an i-cord. Cast on 2 sts and made an i-cord measuring between 80cm (31½in) and 1m (39½in). Fasten off. Roll the i-cord up from the end to make a circle and secure with a few stitches.

Rocks

Cast on 4 sts, k 4 rows. Using the yarn left at the cast-off end, sew the seam. Push the other yarn end inside and close the cast-on end. You do not really need extra stuffing. Place the rocks around the pond and attach them to the mat by sewing.

Materials

DK (8-ply yarn):

For the mat: any colours of your choice. The quantity depends on how big you want the mat to be. To make a mat of 40 x 40cm (16 x 16in), you need about 200g (7oz). Small amounts of green for grass and red, yellow, pink for flowers

For three ponds of 7cm (2¾in) diameter: 25g (1oz) blue

For the rocks: 20g (¾oz) grey or light brown

Needles

A pair of 3mm (UK 11, US 2 or 3) knitting needles

Difficulty level

Beginner

Note

The mat shown opposite, which was used for all the pictures of the completed safari park, is about four times bigger than the size given in the pattern. To make one this size, you would need about 800g (28oz) of yarn. You can vary the sizes by changing the stitches and numbers of rows. You can also use Aran or chunky yarn, or knit with 2 strands of DK (8-ply) yarn. Make crochet clusters instead of knitting the rocks, if you prefer. You can use rocks to fill the little gaps around the pond, or knit small triangular pieces by decreasing the stitches on one side.

Sewing grass on the mat

Thread green yarn. You can use fine 2 or 3-ply yarn if you have it, but DK (8-ply) yarn will also work fine. Pierce the mat from the back, bringing the needle out at the front. Back stitch once to secure the yarn-end. Back stitch the same spot again, leaving a long loop, then back stitch again without leaving a loop. Repeat this process until you are happy with the number of green loops. Cut all the loops to create the grass effect.

Adding flowers

Take any colour of yarn of your choice and make a knot. Hide the yarn-ends inside the knot. Thread a needle with green yarn and pierce the knot. Attach the flower to the mat, where you have sewn the grass. Alternatively, make French knots directly on the mat.

Arched Gateway

Instructions

The vines are crocheted and the eraser covers are knitted.

Vines

With green yarn make 10 ch, miss next ch, ss to the next 1 or 2 ch, make more ch and keep making vine and leaves with this method. Vary the size by increasing or decreasing the number of chains. Make 4 vines, about 25cm (10in) each.

Eraser covers

The ends of the arch are attached to rubber erasers for stability. Each eraser is covered with a knitted piece.

Cast on 10 sts with dark brown yarn.

Rows 1–5: st/st, starting with a k row.

Row 6: k for fold line.

Row 7: Cast on 4, k to end (14).

Row 8: Cast on 4, p to end (18).

Rows 9–11: st/st, starting with a k row.

Row 12: Cast off 4, k to end for fold line (14).

Row 13: Cast off 4, k to end (10).

Rows 14–19: st/st, starting with a p row.

Row 20: k for fold line.

Rows 21–23: st/st, starting with a k row.

Cast off.

Place an eraser inside and sew all the sides, enclosing the eraser completely.

Making up

Wind the dark brown yarn around each length of heavy-duty garden wire, securing it every now and then. Leave 1cm (³⁄₈in) bare at either end. When close to the end, leave several centimetres of yarn for securing the eraser later on.

Place the wires parallel to each other, 2.5cm (1in) apart. Secure them with fine garden wire, zigzagging across and twisting around them.

Decorate with the crocheted vines. Add flower, as for the Safari Mat on pages 80–81.

Press each pair of wire ends into an eraser. Thread a darning needle with the end of the dark brown yarn, push it through the eraser and secure the yarn underneath. Use wire cutters if you find it difficult to pull the needle out of the eraser.

Materials

Two 30cm (11¾in) lengths of heavy-duty green garden wire

60cm (23¾in) fine green garden wire

Two rubber erasers: 1.5 x 3 x 1cm (⅝ x 1¼ x ³⁄₈in)

Craft pliers

DK (8-ply) yarn: small amounts of two shades of green, dark brown, red, white, yellow and pink

Needles

3.25mm (UK 10/US D) crochet hook

Off-Road Vehicle

Instructions

The pattern starts with the bottom piece and moves on to the left side piece, to the roof and to the right side piece, knitted as one. The front piece and the back piece are knitted from stitches picked up from the roof edges.

Bottom piece

With dark brown yarn, cast on 24 sts, and starting with a k row, st/st for 5cm (2in), finishing with a k row.

Next row: k for fold line.

Change to green yarn and continue to the left side.

Left side

Rows 1–9: st/st, starting with a k row.

Row 10: Cast off 7 sts, k to end to create ridge (17).

Row 11: k.

Join in light blue yarn.

Row 12: p2 (green), p4 (light blue) p1 (green), p3 (light blue), p1 (green), p3 (light blue), p3 (green).

Rows 13–15: Keeping the colour pattern correct, st/st.

Row 16: Break off light blue yarn, p with green only.

Row 17: k.

Row 18: k for fold line.

Do not break yarn. Continue to the roof.

Roof

Starting with a k row, st/st for 4cm (1½in), finishing with a k row.

Next row: k for fold line.

Continue to the right side.

Materials

DK (8-ply) yarn: 3g (⅛oz) of dark brown, 15g (½oz) of green and small amounts of light blue, light grey, brown, black and white

Stuffing

Size

9cm (3½in) long, 5cm (2in) high, 6cm (2⅜in) wide

Difficulty level

Advanced

Right side (continued from roof)

Row 1: k.

Row 2: p.

Join in light blue.

Row 3: k3 (green), k3 (light blue), k1 (green), k3 (light blue), k1 (green), k4 (light blue), k2 (green).

Rows 4–6: Keeping the colour pattern correct, st/st.

Row 7: Break off light blue and k with green only.

Row 8: p.

Row 9: p (this creates the ridge, as row 10 on the left side).

Row 10: Cast on 7 sts, p to end (24).

Rows 11–18: st/st, starting with a k row.

Cast off.

Front

With right side facing and green yarn, pick up and k 17 sts from the front roof edge.

Row 1: p.

Join in light blue yarn.

Row 2: k2 (green), k6 (light blue), k1 (green), k6 (light blue), k2 (green).

Rows 3–5: Keeping the colour pattern correct, st/st.

Row 6: Break off light blue yarn, k with green only.

Row 7: k for ridge below window.

Rows 8–20: st/st, starting with a k row.

Row 21: k for fold line.

Rows 22–30: st/st, starting with a k row.

Cast off.

Back

Same as the front up to row 7.
Rows 8–15: st/st, starting with a k row.
Cast off.

Wheels

Small: make two
Cast on 4 sts with black yarn, garter st 22 rows,
change to white yarn, garter st 15 rows. Cast off.
Large: make three
Cast on 4 sts with black yarn, garter st 30 rows,
change to white yarn, garter st 30 rows. Cast off.
Roll up the wheel piece from the white end and secure
with a few stitches, using black yarn.

Headlights: make two

With light grey yarn, cast on 10 sts and k 1 row. Break
yarn, draw it through sts on needle, pull tightly and
fasten off. Following the steps on Making knitted eyes
on page 21, make each headlight into a circle.

Bumper

Cast on 5 sts with light grey yarn and st/st for 8cm
(3in) or just enough to cover the length between the
two front wheels. Cast off.
Alternatively, make a 2-stitch i-cord for 8cm (3in).
Fasten off.

Front grille

Make a 2-stitch i-cord for 4cm (1½in) with light grey
yarn. Fasten off.

Roof rail: make two

Cast on 2 sts in brown yarn and make a 4cm (1½in)
i-cord. Fasten off.

Making up

Sew up the sides and the bottom seam and stuff the
vehicle. Thread a needle with green yarn. From where
the windscreen meets the bonnet (hood), pierce the
vehicle and bring the needle out at the back bottom
seam. Repeat a few times, pulling the thread gently
each time. Attach wheels, headlights, bumper, front
grille and roof rails.

Camper Van

Instructions

The pattern starts with the bottom piece and moves on to the left side piece, the roof and the right side piece, all knitted as one. The front and back pieces are knitted from stitches picked up from the roof edges.

Bottom piece

With white yarn, cast on 24 sts.
Starting with a k row, st/st until work measures 5.5cm (2¼in), finishing with a p row.
Next row: p for fold line.
Break off white yarn and change to red. Continue to left side.

Left side

Rows 1–4: st/st, starting with a p row.
Row 5: p2tog, p to end (23).
Row 6: k.
Row 7: p2tog, p to end (22).
Row 8: k.
Row 9: Join in white, p3 (white), p to end with red.
Row 10: k with red yarn to last 5 sts, k5 (white).
Row 11: Break off red yarn, p all sts with white.
Row 12: p to last 5 sts, k5.
Join in light blue.
Row 13: p2tog, p1 (white) p4 (light blue), p1 (white), p3 (light blue), p1 (white), p3 (light blue), p1 (white), p3 (light blue), p3 (white) (21).
Rows 14–16: Keeping the colour pattern correct, st/st.
Row 17: Break off light blue yarn, p with white.
Row 18: k.
Row 19: k for fold line.

Roof

Starting with a k row, st/st for 3cm (1¼in), finishing with a k row.
Next row: k for fold line.
Continue to the right side.

Right side

Row 1: k.
Join in light blue yarn
Row 2: p2 (white), p4 (light blue), p1 (white), p3 (light blue), p1 (white), p3 (light blue), p1 (white), p3 (light blue), p3 (white).
Rows 3–5: Keeping the colour pattern correct, st/st.
Row 6: Break off light blue yarn, inc 1 st, p to end with white (22).
Row 7: p to last 5, k5.
Row 8: p5 (white), join in red yarn, p to end with red.

Materials

DK (8-ply) yarn: 10g (⅓oz) of red, 10g (⅓oz) of white and small amounts of light blue, light grey and dark brown plus colours of your choice for the embroidery

Stuffing

Size

10cm (4in) long, 7cm (2¾in) wide, 7cm (2¾in) high

Difficulty level

Advanced

Row 9: k with red to last 3 sts, k3 (white).

Row 10: Break off white yarn, p to end with red.

Row 11: k.

Row 12: inc 1 st, p to end (23).

Row 13: k.

Row 14: inc 1 st, p to end (24).

Rows 15–18: st/st.

Cast off.

Front piece

With right side facing and white yarn, pick up and knit13 sts from the front roof edge.

Row 1: p.

Join in light blue.

Row 2: k2 (white), k4 (light blue), k1 (white), k4 (light blue), k2 (white).

Rows 3–5: Keeping the colour pattern correct, st/st.

Row 6: Break off light blue yarn, k with white only.

Row 7: pf/b, p to last st, pf/b (15).

Rows 8–10: st/st.

Row 11: Join in red yarn, p2 (red), p11 (white), p2 (red).

Row 12: k3 (red), k9 (white), k3 (red).

Row 13: pf/b, p3 (red), p7 (white), p3, pf/b (red) (17).

Row 14: k5 (red), k7 (white), k5 (red).

Row 15: pf/b, p5 (red), p5 (white), p5, pf/b (red) (19).

Row 16: k7 (red), k5 (white), k7 (red).

Row 17: p8 (red), p3 (white), p8 (red).

Row 18: k8 (red), k3 (white), k8 (red).

Row 19: p9 (red), p1 (white), p9 (red).

Row 20: Break off white yarn and k with red only.

Cast off.

Back piece

Same as the front piece until row 6.
Row 7: With white yarn, kf/b, k to last st, kf/b for fold line (15).
Rows 8–12: Break off white yarn, st/st with red, starting with a k row.
Row 13: pf/b, p to last st, pf/b (17).
Row 14: k.
Row 15: pf/b, p15, pf/b (19).
Rows 16–20: st/st.
Cast off.

Wheels: make four

Cast on 3 sts with dark brown yarn.
Garter stitch for 22 rows. Change to white yarn and garter stitch a further 20 rows.
Cast off.

Bumper

Using pale grey, cast on 6 sts and st/st for 10cm (4in).
Cast off.

Top luggage carrier

With white yarn, cast on 12 sts and st/st 12 rows. Cast off.

Headlights: make two

Cast on 10 sts with light grey yarn and k 1 row. Break yarn, draw it through sts on needle, pull tightly and fasten off. Following the steps on Making knitted eyes on page 21, make each headlight into a circle.

Making up

Tidy up the yarn ends by hiding them inside. You do not need to cut the yarn-ends, since they will all go inside the van. Sew up all the sides and stuff and shape. Roll up the wheel piece from the white end and secure with a few stitches of dark brown yarn. Attach wheels, headlights and bumper to the van. Sew the long sides of the top luggage carrier to the roof. Embroider flowers on the sides and a peace sign in the centre of the front piece, following the patterns on page 19.

Overleaf
The complete knitted safari on the safari mat.

Details from the safari park.